A Time to Dance

Celebrating 400 years of the
King James Version of the Bible

S. T. R. Gamble

The title of this book is from Ecclesiastes Chapter 3, Verse 4 "*A time to weep, and a time to laugh; a time to mourn, and a time to dance*"

Slieve Croob Press
Northern Ireland

First published in 2011 by Slieve Croob, available in the United Kingdom and Republic of Ireland from Slieve Croob Press, and worldwide through the Internet.

Copyright © 2011 S.T.R. Gamble

ISBN: 978-1-4475-4025-0

Printed and bound in the United Kingdom of Great Britain and Northern Ireland.

This book is sold subject to the condition that it shall not, by way of trade or otherwise, be lent, re-sold, hired out or otherwise circulated without the publisher's prior consent in any form of binding or cover other than that in which it is published and without a similar condition including this condition being imposed on the subsequent purchaser.

All rights reserved. No part of this publication may be reproduced, stored in a retrieval system, or transmitted, in any form or by any means, electronic, mechanical, photocopying, or otherwise, without the prior permission of the publishers.

In thanks for Grace

Contents

Foreword	*S.E. Long*	7
Introduction		15
The Accession of King James 1		21
The Hampton Court Conference		29
The Translation Process		37
On the Shoulders of Giants		45
The Gift of the King James Version		51
Appendix 1		59
The Confession of King James 1		
Appendix 2		83
To the Most High and Mighty Prince James		

Foreword

S.E. LONG

The 400th Anniversary of the publication of the King James Bible, the Authorised Version - is being much marked because of the pivotal place it holds in the thinking and living of Christians and all others who highly value it for whatever reason.

This is being done by Bible centred pageants and exhibitions, through essays, books, and by the media in sound and vision. I am delighted that this book, which resulted from invitations to lecture on the subject, contributes to the celebrations. It will give you an introduction to the history underlying the King James Bible.

The Holy Bible has been described as the great unread, international bestseller. Reasons were given for this anomaly, for while many people have a Bible in their homes it is often left unread. That as some have said, is because while lists of it are easy to read much of it is difficult to understand for the literary style is old fashioned and unfamiliar.

That objection of the Authorised Version has little relevance now for modem translations have, made the Bible easy to read for most literate people. Their appearance in the format of books generally removes the objection that leather binding, onion skin paper and the "mysteriousness" of the Bible made it "too exalted to be consulted."

To describe the Bible simply is to say it is a book about God and His dealings with people from it we learn many things about the ancient world, the aspirations and experiences of a nation; the hopes and fears, attitudes, actions and desires of some extraordinary and many ordinary people.

There are incomparable gems of wisdom in prose and poetry that come out of the deeps of human emotions. It deals with the problems that confront people, personal, familial and in community. It is described properly as a treasure house of revelation, information, knowledge and experience.

Important and invaluable as these are, the Bible is not just a compendium of useful data a bank to be used for specific purpose:-. It should not be seen as some might see a great cathedral to admire its architecture, rejoice in its music, delight in its magnificent artefacts and furnishings and miss the real reason for its use for it is the House of God in which He is worshipped and the worth and work of Christ is recognised and proclaimed.

The specific task of the church is to encourage and enable people to have communion with God and fellowship with others who have similar intention.

The primary use of the Bible is to describe God as loving and caring, willing to supply the needs of people, for He wants only our good.

The Old Testament emphasises the righteousness, justice and mercy of God.

The New Testament emphasises the intervention of God in human history in the Person and work of Jesus Christ.

The Bible constantly reminds us that Christianity is Christ. Its timeless value is evidenced in that it addresses the most pressing and continuous needs, aims and aspirations of people. CH Spurgeon said "No one ever outgrows Scripture; it widens and deepens with our years."

The Bible teaches us about God and encourages us to have faith in Him, to be obedient to Him and to be kind to one another. It is the ground of hope for it provides comfort and consolation when time and experience bring much to dishearten and confuse us. The hope it engenders will keep the heart safe from the doubts which enslave the mind and shatter the body, it is in God as He reveals Himself and especially in the person and work of Jesus.

The Bible is "God's ordinary means of conversation with people." Alan Richardson said in explanation:

"'If God speaks to men through the Church it is because the church is the place where the Bible is read and the community which listens to the public reading of the Bible. If God speaks to men through the sacraments it is because they are the sacraments of the Bible drama. If God speaks to men in the sermon it is because the Bible is preached. If God speaks to men in prayer it is because it is stimulated by what the Bible says on the subject."

The power of the Bible to influence mind, motive, heart and conscience in everything to do with truth, purity and generosity cannot be overstated and it is, given the opportunity, the spur to conscience.

CH. Spurgeon with an evangelist's bluntness said; "If God is a reality and the soul is a reality and you are an immortal being, what arc you doing with your Bible shut?"

"Blessed are they who hear the Word of God and keep it." (Luke 11:28)

Rev. Canon Dr. S.E. Long

April 2011

Introduction

This year is the 400th Anniversary of the King James Version of the Bible. In 1611, the first Authorised Version of the Bible appeared and the rest you could say is history.

And what a history there has been in between. There has been the Civil War between Charles 1 and Oliver Cromwell, the Restoration of the Monarchy 1660, and the Glorious Revolution of 1688-1690. There has been the growth of Britain as a world cultural and economic power, the rise and fall of the British Empire, the First and Second World Wars, the Cold War and the rise and fall of Communism.

There has also been the long and happy reign of our current monarch, Queen Elizabeth 11, who God willing will celebrate her Diamond Jubilee, next year. And at Christmas, it was heartening to see her take the lead in marking this important milestone in the life of our nation – 400 years of the King James Bible. In her Christmas Day speech, Her Majesty said:

"Over four hundred years ago, King James the Sixth of Scotland inherited the throne of England at a time when the Christian Church was deeply divided. Here at Hampton Court in 1604, he convened a conference of churchmen of all shades of opinion to discuss the future of Christianity in this country. The King agreed to commission a new translation of the Bible that was acceptable to all parties. This was to become the King James or Authorized Bible, which next year will be exactly four centuries old.

Acknowledged as a masterpiece of English prose and the most vivid translation of the scriptures, the glorious language of this Bible has survived the turbulence of history and given many of us the most widely-recognised and beautiful descriptions of the birth of Jesus Christ which we celebrate today.

Her Majesty Queen Elizabeth 11, *Queen of the United Kingdom of Great Britain and Northern Ireland, Defender of the Faith.*

The King James Bible was a major cooperative endeavour that required the efforts of dozens of the day's leading scholars. The whole enterprise was guided by an interest in reaching agreement for the wider benefit of the Christian Church, and to bring harmony to the Kingdoms of England and Scotland."

It's heartening to read such clear and meaningful words from HM Queen, reminding us all that at the heart of our Constitution lies a strong commitment to the Gospel of our Lord Jesus Christ, and that, on the British throne, sits a committed and faithful Protestant, who has been exemplary in her service, not least in the lead which she has taken in marking 400 years of the King James Bible.

It also reminds us that the King James Bible has played a significant and substantial role in the life and history of our nation. It has shaped our culture and art, music and language, politics and people. It has been used as much in Society as in Church. Generation after generation have known the King James Version quite simply as the Holy Bible, to be read, revered, respected and reflected upon.

In light of this, I want to look briefly at the history of the King James Bible by asking the following questions: How did it come about? Who was King James 1? Who were the main players at that time? Why did the Hampton Court Conference take place? Who took part in the translation? And what did they give us in translation?

The Accession of King James 1

Elizabeth 1, "Good Queen Bess" as she is known, died in 1603 after a long and successful reign. She had brought much stability to the nation, restoring Protestantism as the official religion, seeing off the threat of the Spanish Armada, and overseeing a Golden Age of economic growth and development. So when news of her death spread, there was great sorrow and sadness. Elizabeth is also known as "the Virgin Queen". She never married and therefore did not produce a Protestant heir to throne. So when it came to the issue of a Protestant successor, there was much concern. Who could succeed Elizabeth and secure the throne and life of the nation?

The eyes of many fell upon the son of Mary Queen of Scots, who had ascended the Scottish throne in 1567. James Vl had shown himself to be a staunch supporter of Protestantism in Scotland, and therefore could be relied upon to safeguard Elizabeth's Protestant legacy.

And so in 1603, James Vl of Scotland, became James 1 of England. He was male, Protestant, possessed both rank and experience of government. He had a strong hereditary claim to the English throne, and already had children – so the question of who would succeed James would not be as difficult as it was with Elizabeth.

To the Puritans of England, the succession of James was good news, or so they thought. He had maintained a Presbyterian system of government in the Church of Scotland, and their hope was that he would bring some of this Presbyterianism, if not all of it, south with him to England.

Under Elizabeth 1, a Protestant Episcopacy had been restored and maintained. The Church of England was governed by Bishops and her services came from the Book of Common Prayer.

His Majesty King James 1, *King of Great Britain, France and Ireland, Defender of the Faith.*

In Scotland, however, the situation was very different. Episcopacy and the Book of Common Prayer had been shown the ecclesiastical door by John Knox, and a Presbyterian system of government, and a Presbyterian system of worship was in place.

For the English Puritans, who wanted to see the Church of England further reformed, more like the Church of Scotland, the news of a new king had raised great hopes and expectations.

There was no doubt that James was a clear and committed Protestant. In his confession of faith, James had set out a strongly Reformed and Catholic position. As a Protestant, he boldly asserted that he was a "Catholic Christian", who believed in the historic Christian faith. By catholic, he meant the faith as believed everywhere by everyone from the time of Christ and the Apostles. He did not understand it in a denominational sense, as it is popularly understood today. By outlining his catholicity, James was defending the authenticity of his Protestant faith.

However, the Puritans had misread their new King. Far from being a "Puritan King", James was fearful of Presbyterianism. He believed passionately that his royal authority was dependent on bishops. His reasoning was "no bishops, no king." Yes he had publicly supported the Presbyterian system in Scotland, but privately he had misgivings.

He had misgivings about the Geneva Bible, which Presbyterians were using. It wasn't so much the translation of the Bible which concerned him, but the marginal notes, which were to aid the reading of the

Bible. Some of the notes, or accompanying comments, could easily be read as advocating republicanism, and this alarmed James. So a new translation of the Bible without political footnotes and comments was very much on his wish list.

The Hampton Court Conference 1604

On 24th October 1603, James issued a proclamation stating that he was convening a conference to be attended by himself, the Privy Council, and various bishops and learned men to deal with the religious issues of that time.

This conference, the Hampton Court Conference, was to prove decisive in bringing about the King James Version of the Bible.

Initially, it created high hopes for the Puritans. Here was their chance for a Puritan Church and a Puritan nation, or so they thought.

The Bishops of the Church of England were alarmed. How could they protect what they held to dearly, the Episcopacy and the Prayer Book?

When the Conference opened, it was heavily weighted toward the established Church. The future Archbishop of Canterbury, Richard Bancroft, was joined by the bishops of Carlisle, Chichester, Durham, Peterborough, St. David's, Winchester, and

Worcester. The six cathedral deans present included the deans of Westminster Abbey and St. Paul's Cathedral. When the king's Privy Council is taken into account, there were nineteen representatives of the establishment, and only four Puritans.

The Puritans were John Reynolds, who was President of Corpus Christi College, Oxford; Laurence Chadderton, who was Master of Emmanuel College, Cambridge; John Knewstubs, Fellow of St. John's College Cambridge, and Thomas Sparke, Minister of Bletchley in Buckinghamshire.

The Conference was opened with an hour long speech by King James. In it, he said that he was happy with the established religion and didn't wish to change it. Yet he also gave some room for Putiran reforms.

"I assure you we have not called this assembly for any innovation, for we acknowledge the government ecclesiastical as it now is, to have been approved by manifolds blessings from God himself, both for the increase of the Gospel, and with a most happy and glorious peace. Yet because nothing can be so absolutely ordered, but something may be added thereunto, and corruption in any state (as in the body of man) will insensibly grow either through time or persons, and because we have many complaints sine our first entrance into this kingdom, of many disorders, and much disobedience to the laws, with a great falling away to popery; our purpose therefore is, like a good physician, to examine and try the complaints and fully remove occasions

A Time To Dance: Celebrating 400 years of the King James Bible

thereof, if scandalous; cure them, if dangerous."

As good physicians, what did they look at? To begin with they looked at three things.

1. The Book of Common Prayer.
2. Excommunication
3. The providing of fit and able ministers for Ireland.

One humorous account, resulted when John Reynolds objected to the phrase in the Marriage Service, "with my body, I thee worship." For him, this went against the commandment that only God should be worshipped, and therefore needed to be changed.

James responded with the quip, "If you had a good wife yourself, you would think all the honour and worship you would do her were well bestowed!"

The conference was not going well for the Puritans, but James did not want them to go away empty handed. He reasoned that if Episcopacy and the Prayer Book remained, then some concession would have to be made to the Puritans.

The breakthrough came when John Reynolds, the Puritan, proposed a new translation of the Bible. The King was open to this proposal, even if the leading bishop, Richard Bancroft was not.

Here was a major concession that could be made to the Puritans by the King, a concession which had the potential to unite his subjects around an authorised version of the Bible.

Thus James directed that "the best learned in both universities" should produce a new translation of the Bible, which would be reviewed by the bishops and learned men, before being presented to the Privy Council and finally ratified by royal authority, so that the whole church would be bound to it, and none other."

And so the resolution was passed that "a translation be made of the whole Bible, as consonant as can be to the original Hebrew and Greek; and this to be set out and printed, without marginal notes, and only to be used in all churches of England in time of divine service."

The Translation Process

The universities of Oxford and Cambridge got to work along with Westminster Abbey, guided by the translation rules of Bishop Bancroft. Remember he was initially opposed to a new Bible at the Conference because he feared change, but now he was able to steer the translation process with some necessary safeguards in place to protect the established religion.

The Rules to be observed in the Translation of the Bible, where as follows:
1. The ordinary Bible read in the Church, commonly called the Bishops Bible, to be followed, and as little altered as the Truth of the original will permit.

2. The Names of the Prophets, and the Holy Writers, with the other Names of the Text, to be retained, as nigh as may be, accordingly as they were vulgarly used.

3. The old Ecclesiastical Words to be kept, viz. the Word Church not to be translated Congregation &c.

4. When a Word hath divers Significations; that to be kept which hath been most commonly used by the most of the Ancient Fathers, being agreeable to the Propriety of the Place, and the Analogy of the Faith.

5. The Divisions of the Chapters to be altered, either not at all, or as little as may be, if Necessity so require.

6. No Marginal Notes at all to be affixed, but only for the Explanation of the Hebrew or Greek Words, which cannot, without some circumlocution, so briefly and fitly be express'd in the Text.

7. Such Quotations of Places to marginally set down as shall serve for the fit Reference of one Scripture to another.

Most Rev. Richard Bancroft, *Archbishop of Canterbury*

8. Every particular Man of each Company, to take the same Chapter, or Chapters, and having translated or amended them severally by himself, where he thinketh good, all to meet together, confer what they have done, and agree for their Parts what shall stand.

9. As any one Company hath dispatched any one Book in this manner they shall send it to the rest, to be consider'd of seriously and judiciously, for His Majesty is very careful in this Point.

10. If any Company, upon the Review of the Book so sent, doubt or differ upon any Place, to send them Word thereof; note the Place, to send them Word thereof; note the Place and withal send the Reasons, to which if they consent not, the Difference to be compounded at the General Meeting, which

is to be of the chief Persons of each Company, at the end of the Work.

11. When any Place of special Obscurity is doubted of, Letters to be directed, by Authority, to send to any Learned Man in the Land, for his Judgement of such a Place.

12. Letters to be sent from every Bishop to the rest of his Clergy, admonishing them of this Translation in hand; and to move and charge as many as being skilful in the Tongues; and having taken Pains in that kind, to send his particular Observations to the Company, either at Westminster, Cambridge or Oxford.

13. The directors in each Company, to be the Deans of Westminster and Chester for that Place; and the King's Professors in the Hebrew or Greek in either University.

14. These Translations to be used when they agree better with the Text than the Bishop's Bible; Tindoll's, Matthew's, Coverdale's, Whitechurch's, Geneva.

15. Besides the said Directors before mentioned, three of four of the most Ancient and Grave Divines, in either of the Universities, not employed in Translating, to be assigned by the vice- Chancellor, upon Conference with the rest of the Heads, to be Overseers of the Translations as well as Hebrew and Greek, for the better observation of the 4th Rule above specified.

With these rules in place, six different companies or groups set to work on the new Bible.

The First Westminster Company, headed by Lancelot Andrewes, translated the first part of the Old Testament, Genesis to 2 Kings. The First Cambridge Company, worked on 1 Chronicles to Song of Songs. The First Oxford company, headed by John Harding, President of Magdalen College, worked on Isaiah to Malachi. The Second Oxford company, translated the Gospels, Acts and Revelation. The Second Westminster Company, worked on the New Testament letters. And the Second Cambridge Company worked on the Apocryphal books.

After seven years of careful and painstaking work, the translation process was complete. Britain had finally received the much loved King James Version of the Bible.

On the Shoulders of Giants

It must be noted that, in many ways, the King James Version was not entirely a new translation of the Bible. The translators in Cambridge, Oxford and Westminster were standing on the shoulders of giants.

Building on the advances in Hebrew and Greek scholarship, together with the insights of previous translators, the translation teams produced a remarkably rich and resonant version, which was to serve for public readings in churches as well as private devotional reading. The Bishop of Gloucester, Miles Smith, wrote the Preface, which acknowledged the new translation's debt to its predecessors, but set out the hope that "out of many good ones" there would now be "one principal good one" used by everyone.

Therefore, as we celebrate the 400th anniversary of the King James Version of the Bible, it is important to remember all the translators and translations that have gone before it, right the way back to John Wycliffe and the Lollards.

They were forerunners of the Reformation in England, calling for reforms and advocating the Bible in the language of the people. Wycliffe translated the Scriptures from the Latin Vulgate into vernacular English in 1382. It became known as Wycliffe's Bible.

We should especially remember the Protestant martyr, William Tyndale and his efforts to have the Word of God in the mother tongue. Tyndale was an academic scholar and bible translator, who became a leading figure among early English Protestants. Influenced by the work of Erasmus, who made the Greek New Testament available in Europe, and Martin Luther, who kick-started the Reformation, he was the first to translate considerable parts of the Bible into English.

William Tyndale, *Protestant Martyr and Bible Translator*

Tyndale's was the first English translation to draw directly from the original Hebrew and Greek texts. Furthermore, he was the first to take advantage of the new printing press, which allowed mass distribution and readership.

In 1535, Tyndale was arrested by the Catholic Church authorities and jailed in the castle of Vilvoorde outside Brussels for over a year. He was tried for heresy, strangled and burnt at the stake in 1536.

Tyndale's final words, spoken "at the stake with a fervent zeal, and a loud voice", were "Lord! Open the King of England's eyes." Within four years, this payer had been answered. At the behest of King Henry V111, four English translations were published in England, all based on Tyndale's work. His translation, was followed by Matthew's Bible, Coverdale's Bible, Whitchurch's Bible, the Bishop's Bible and we must not forget the Geneva Bible.

All of these previous translations were used by the King James translators, and helped to shape and mould the Authorised Version of the Bible as printed in 1611.

The King James Bible translators were very much standing on the shoulders of giants, and they had no hesitation in admitting so. It's only right then, that we should remember and celebrate those giants of old as well, and give thanks to God for their contribution.

The Gift of the King James Version

After exploring the history underlying the King James Version of the Bible, it is important for us to pause and ask ourselves the question: what did the King James translators give us in translation?

Firstly, they gave us a translation with phrases such as:

> "the salt of the earth"
>
> "the powers that be"
>
> " a law unto themselves"
>
> "all things to all men"
>
> "signs of the times"
>
> "suffer fools gladly"
>
> "a howling wilderness"
>
> "the straight and narrow"
>
> "nothing new under the sun"
>
> " a land flowing with milk and honey"
>
> " a man after his own heart"
>
> "the leopard cannot change his spots."

"wheels within wheels"

" an eye for an eye"

"turn the other cheek"

"a time and a place for everything"

"all the days of my life"

These phrases have entered into everyday English, and remain in popular usage, even if many who use them do not know, or cite their original source.

Secondly, they gave us a translation with poetry such as this:

Psalm 23

[1]The LORD is my shepherd; I shall not want.

²He maketh me to lie down in green pastures: he leadeth me beside the still waters.

³He restoreth my soul: he leadeth me in the paths of righteousness for his name's sake.

⁴Yea, though I walk through the valley of the shadow of death, I will fear no evil: for thou art with me; thy rod and thy staff they comfort me.

⁵Thou preparest a table before me in the presence of mine enemies: thou anointest my head with oil; my cup runneth over.

⁶Surely goodness and mercy shall follow me all the days of my life: and I will dwell in the house of the LORD for ever.

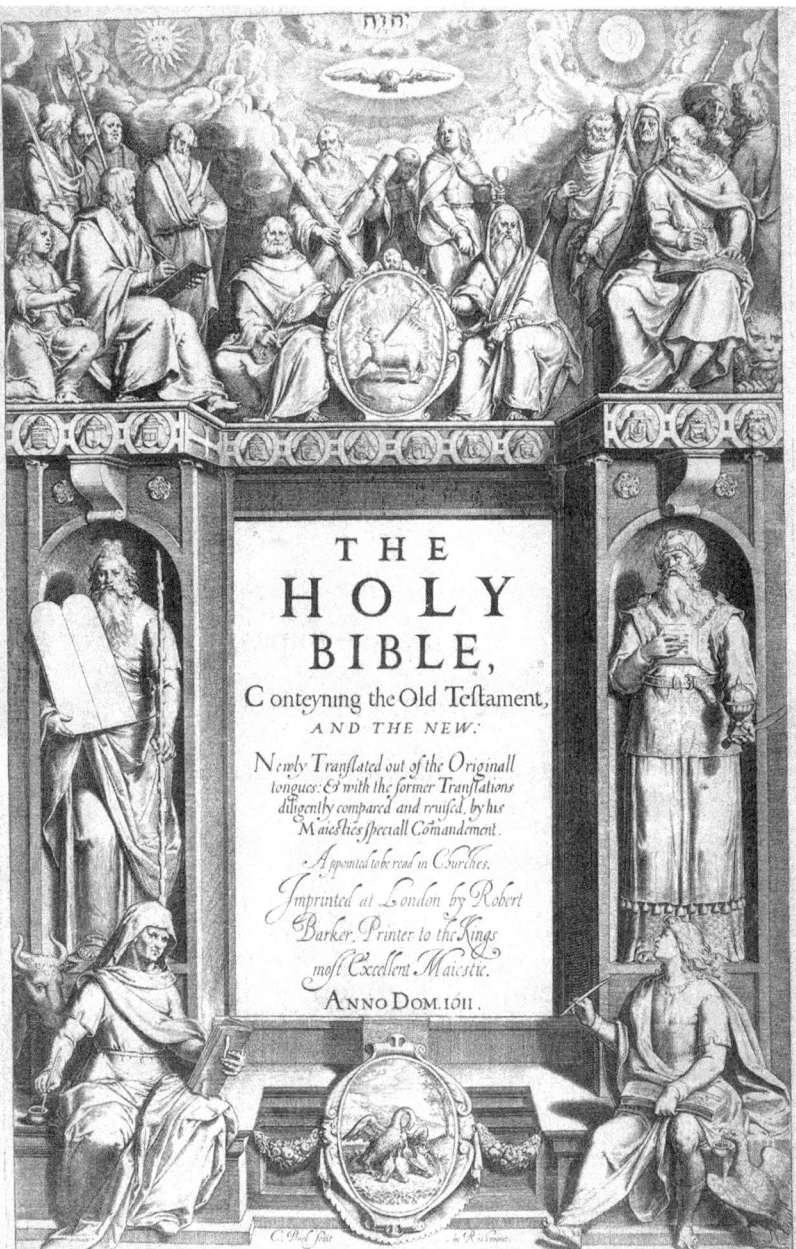

Frontispiece to the King James Bible, 1611.

These words capture the essence of the Hebrew psalm so wonderfully. They have been a source of much comfort and great strength to many, especially at times of bereavement.

Thirdly, they gave us a translation with history rendered like this:

Luke 2

1 And it came to pass in those days, that there went out a decree from Caesar Augustus that all the world should be taxed.

2 (And this taxing was first made when Cyrenius was governor of Syria.)

3 And all went to be taxed, every one into his own city.

4 And Joseph also went up from Galilee, out of the city of Nazareth, into

Judaea, unto the city of David, which is called Bethlehem; (because he was of the house and lineage of David:)

5 To be taxed with Mary his espoused wife, being great with child.

6 And so it was, that, while they were there, the days were accomplished that she should be delivered.

7 And she brought forth her firstborn son, and wrapped him in swaddling clothes, and laid him in a manger; because there was no room for them in the inn.

For many, these words make Christmas what it is. They have produced a sense of wonder, mystery and amazement at countless carol services and school nativity plays throughout the country.

And finally, they gave us a translation with the most well known verse of all, rendered as this:

John 3:16

> ^{16}For God so loved the world that he gave his only begotten Son, that whosoever believeth in him should not perish, but have everlasting life.

This verse, which sums up the Christian gospel in a nutshell, has been memorised and quoted as such by millions of Christians throughout the world for four centuries.

Quite simply, they gave us a Bible in the English language that has become part of our cultural and religious fabric, part of our way of life, part of our very being itself. And for this, we give thanks to God! "O give thanks unto the LORD; for he is good: for his mercy endureth for ever." (Psalm 136)

Appendix 1

The Confession of King James 1

I will never be ashamed to render an accompt of my profession and of that hope that is in me, as the Apostle prescribeth. I am such a CATHOLIC CHRISTIAN as believeth the three Creeds, that of the Apostles, that of the

Council of Nice, and that of Athanasius, the two latter being paraphrases to the former. And I believe them in that sense as the ancient Fathers and Councils that made them did understand them, to which three Creeds all the ministers of England do subscribe at their Ordination. And I also acknowledge for Orthodox all those other forms of Creeds that either were devised by Councils or particular Fathers, against such particular heresies as most reigned in their times.

I reverence and admit the Four First General Councils as Catholic and Orthodox. And the said Four General Councils are acknowledged by our Acts of Parliament, and received for orthodox by our Church.

As for the Fathers, I reverence them as much and more than the Jesuits do, and as much as themselves ever craved. For whatever the Fathers for the first five hundred years did with an unanime consent agree upon, to be believed as a necessary point of salvation, I either will believe it also, or at least will be humbly silent, not taking upon me to condemn the same. But for every private Father's opinion, it binds not my conscience more than Bellarmine's, every one of the Fathers usually contradicting others. I will therefore in that case follow St. Augustine's rule in judging of their opinions as I find them agree with the Scriptures. What I find agreeable thereto I will gladly embrace. What is otherwise I will (with their reverence) reject.

As for the Scriptures, no man doubteth I will believe them. But even for the Apocrypha, I hold them in the same accompt that the Ancients did. They are still printed and bound with our Bibles, and publicly read in our churches. I reverence them as the writings of holy and good men. But since they are not found in the Canon, we accompt them to be *secundae lectionis* or *ordinis* (which is Bellarmine's own distinction) and therefore not sufficient whereupon alone to ground any Article of Faith, except it be confirmed by some other place of Canonical Scripture; concluding this point with Rufinus (who is no Novelist, I hope) that the Apocryphal books were by the Fathers permitted to be read, not for confirmation of doctrine, but only for instruction of the people.

As for the Saints departed, I honour their memory, and in honour of them do we in our Church observe the days of so many of them as the Scripture doth canonize for saints; but I am loath to believe all the tales of the legended saints.

And first for the Blessed Virgin Mary, I yield her that which the Angel Gabriel pronounced of her, and which in her Canticle she prophecied of herself, that is, That she is blessed among women, and That all generations shall call her blessed. I reverence her as the Mother of Christ, of whom our Saviour took His flesh, and so the Mother of God, since the Divinity and Humanity of Christ are inseparable. And I freely confess that she is in glory both above angels and men, her own Son (that is both God and man) only excepted. But I dare not mock her, and blaspheme against God, calling her not only *Diva* but *Dea,* and praying her to command and control her Son, Who is her God and her Saviour. Nor yet not, I think, that she hath no other thing to do in Heaven than to hear every idle man's suit and busy herself in their errands, whiles requesting, whiles commanding her

Son, whiles coming down to kiss and make love with priests, and whiles disputing and brawling with devils. In Heaven she is in eternal glory and joy, never to be interrupted with any worldly business; and there I leave her with her blessed Son, our Saviour and hers, in eternal felicity.

As for prayer to Saints, Christ, I am sure, hath commanded us to come all to Him that are loaden with sin, and He will relieve us; and St. Paul hath forbidden us to worship angels, or to use any such voluntary worship, that hath a shew of humility in that it spareth not the flesh. But what warrant we have to have recourse unto these *Dii Penates* or *Tutelares,* these Courtiers of God, I know not; I remit that to these philosophical Neoteric Divines. It satisfieth me to pray to God through Christ, as I am commanded, which I am sure must be the safest way; and

I am sure the safest way is the best way in points of salvation. But if the Romish Church hath coined new Articles of Faith, never heard of in the first 500 years after Christ, I hope I shall never be condemned for an heretic, for not being a Novelist. Such are the Private Masses, where the Priest playeth the part both of the Priest and of the People. And such are the Amputation of the one half of the Sacrament from the people; the Transubstantiation, Elevation for Adoration, and Circumportation in procession of the Sacrament; the Works of Supererogation, rightly named *Thesaurus Ecclesiae;* the Baptizing of Bells and a thousand other tricks, but above all, the Worshipping of Images. If my faith be weak in these, I confess I had rather believe too little than too much. And yet since I believe as much as the Scriptures do warrant, the Creeds do persuade, and the ancient

Councils decreed, I may well be a schismatic from Rome, but I am sure I am no heretic.

For Relics of Saints, If I had any such I were assured were members of their bodies, I would honourably bury them and not give them the reward of condemned men's members, which are only ordained to be deprived of burial. But for worshipping either them or images, I must account it damnable idolatry.

I am no Iconomachus. I quarrel not with the making of images, either for public decoration or for men's private uses. But that they should be worshipped, be prayed to, or any holiness attributed unto them, was never known of the ancients. And the Scriptures are so directly, vehemently, and punctually against it, as I wonder what brain of man or suggestion of Satan durst offer it to

Christians. And all must be salved with nice philosophical distinctions as Idolunt nihil est; and They worship (forsooth) the Images of things in being and the Image of the true God. But the Scripture forbiddeth to worship the Image of anything that God created. It was not a nihil then that God forbade only to be worshipped, neither was the Brazen Serpent nor the body of Moses a nihil; and yet the one was destroyed and the other hidden for eschewing of idolatry. Yea, the Image of God Himself is not only expressly forbidden to be worshipped, but even to be made. The reason is given, That no eye ever saw God; and how can we paint His Face, when Moses (the man that was ever most familiar with God) never saw but His back parts? Surely, since He cannot be drawn to the vive, it is a thankless labour to mar it with a false representation; which no Prince, nor scarcely any other man, will be contented with in their own pictures. Let them therefore that maintain this doctrine answer it to Christ at the latter day, when He shall accuse them of idolatry. And then I doubt if He will be paid with such nice sophistical distinctions....

As for Purgatory, and all the trash depending thereupon, it is not worth the talking of; Bellarmine cannot find any ground for it in all the Scriptures. Only I would pray him to tell me, If that fair green meadow that is in Purgatory have a brook running through it, that in case I come there I may have hawking upon it. But as for me, I am sure there is a Heaven and a Hell, *praenium et poena*, for the Elect and Reprobate; how many other rooms there be, I am not on God His council. *Multae sunt mansiones in domo Patris mei*, ["there are many mansions in my father's house"] saith

Christ, Who is the true purgatory for our sins. But how many chambers and antechambers the Devil hath, they can best tell that go to him. But in case there were more places for souls to go to than we know of, yet let us content us with that which in His Word He hath revealed unto us, and not inquire further into His secrets. Heaven and Hell are there revealed to be the eternal home of all mankind. Let us endeavour to win the one and eschew the other; and there is an end.

Now in all this discourse have I yet left out the main article of the Romish faith, and that is, the Head of the Church or Peter's Primacy; for who denieth this, denieth *fidem Catholicam* [The catholic faith], saith Bellarmine. That Bishops ought to be in the Church, I ever maintained it as an Apostolic institution and so the ordinance of

God, contrary to the Puritans, and likewise to Bellarmine, who denies that Bishops have their jurisdiction immediately from God. (But it is no wonder he takes the Puritans' part, since Jesuits are nothing but Puritan-Papists.) And as I ever maintained the state of Bishops and the Ecclesiastical Hierarchy for order sake, so was I ever an enemy to the confused anarchy or parity of the Puritans, as well appeareth in my *Basilikon Archon*. Heaven is governed by order, and all the good angels there. Nay, Hell itself could not subsist without some order. And the very devils are divided into legions and have their chieftains. How can any society, then, upon earth subsist without order and degrees? And therefore I cannot enough wonder with what brazen face this Answerer could say, That I was a Puritan in Scotland and an enemy to Protestants, - I that was persecuted by Puritans there, not from my birth only, but even since four months before my birth? I that in the year of God 84 [1584] I erected Bishops and depressed all their popular parity, I then being not 18 years of age? I that in my said Book to my Son do speak ten times more bitterly of them nor of the Papists, having in my second edition thereof affixed a long Apologetic Preface, only *in odium Puritanorum?* And I that for the space of six years before my coming into England laboured nothing so much as to depress their parity and re-erect Bishops again? Nay, if the daily commentaries of my life and actions in Scotland were written (as Julius Caesar's were) there would scarcely a month pass in all my life, since my entering into the thirteenth year of my age, wherein some accident or other would not convince the Cardinal of a lie in this point. And surely I give a fair commendation to the Puritans in that place of my book, where I affirm that I have found greater honesty with the highland and border thieves than with that sort of people. But leaving him to his own impudence, I return to my purpose.

Of Bishops and Church Hierarchy I very well allow (as I said before) and likewise of ranks and degrees amongst bishops. Patriarchs I know were in the time of the Primitive Church, and I likewise reverence that institution for order sake; and amongst them was a contention for the first place. And for myself (if that were yet the question) I would with all my heart give my consent that the Bishop of Rome should have the first seat; I being a Western King would go with the Patriarch of the West. And for his temporal principality over the Signory of Rome, I do not quarrel it either. Let him in God His Name be *Primus Episcopus inter omnes Episcopos* ["first bishop among all bishops"], and *Princeps Episcoporum* [Prince of bishops] so it be no otherwise but as Peter was *Princeps Apostolorum*. But as I well allow of the hierarchy of the Church for distinction of orders (for so I understand it), so I utterly deny that there is an earthly Monarch thereof, whose word must be a law, and who cannot err in his sentence, by an Infallibility of Spirit. Because earthly Kingdoms must have earthly Monarchs, it doth not follow that the Church must have a visible Monarch too. For the world hath not one earthly temporal Monarch. Christ is His Church's Monarch, and the Holy Ghost His Deputy, *Reges Gentium dominants eorum, vos autem non sic.* Christ did not promise before His Ascension to leave Peter with them to direct and instruct them in all things. But He promised to send the Holy Ghost unto them for that end.

And as for these two before cited places, whereby Bellarmine maketh the Pope to triumph over kings, I mean *Pasce oves* and *Tibi dabo claves,* the Cardinal knows well enough that the same words of *Tibi dabo* are in another place spoken by Christ in the plural number. And he likewise knows what reason the ancients do give why Christ bade Peter *pascere oves,* and also what a cloud of witnesses there is, both of ancients, and even of late Popish writers, yea divers Cardinals, that do all agree, that both these speeches used to Peter were meant to all the Apostles represented in his person. Otherwise, how could Paul direct the Church of Corinth to excommunicate the incestuous person *cum spiritu* suo, whereas he should then have said, *cum spiritu Petri?* And how could all the Apostles have otherwise used all their censures only in Christ's Name, and never a word of His Vicar? Peter, we read, did in all the Apostles' meetings sit amongst them as one of their number. And when chosen men were sent to Antiochia from that great Apostolic Council at Jerusalem *(Acts* xv), the text saith, *It seemed good to the Apostles and Elders with the whole Church to send chosen men;* but no mention made of the Head thereof. And so in their Letters no mention is made of Peter, but only of the Apostles, Elders, and Brethren. And it is a wonder why Paul rebuketh the Church of Corinth for making exception of persons, because some followed Paul, some Apollos, some Cephas, if Peter was their visible Head! For then those that followed not Peter or Cephas renounced the Catholic Faith. But it appeareth well that Paul knew little of our new doctrine, since he handleth Peter so rudely, as he not only compareth, but preferreth, himself unto him. But our

Cardinal proves Peter's superiority by Paul's going to visit him. Indeed Paul saith, He went to Jerusalem to visit Peter and confer with him. But he should have added, "And to kiss his feet." . . .

Thus have I now made a free Confession of my Faith. And, I hope, I have fully cleared myself from being an Apostate; and, as far from being an heretic as one may be, that believeth the Scriptures, and the three Creeds, and acknowledgeth the four first General Councils. If I be loath to believe too much, especially of novelties, men of greater knowledge may well pity my weakness. But I am sure none will condemn me for an heretic, save such as make the Pope their God, and think him such a speaking Scripture as they can define heresy no otherwise, but to be whatsoever opinion is maintained against the Pope's definition of faith. And I will sincerely promise, that whenever any point of the Religion I profess shall be proved to be new, and not Ancient, Catholic, and Apostolic (I mean for matter of faith), I will as soon renounce it, closing up this head with the maxim of Vincentius Lirinensis, that I will never refuse to embrace any opinion in divinity necessary to salvation which the whole Catholic Church with an unanime consent have constantly taught and believed even from the Apostles' days, for the space of many ages thereafter without any interruption.[1]

---

[1] From *A Premonition to All Most Mighty Monarchs, Kings, Free Princes, and States of Christendom Works*, ed. James Montague, Bp. of Wint hester (1616), pp. 301-308.

Appendix 2

To the Most High and Mighty Prince James, By The Grace of God

The translators of the Bible wish Grace, Mercy, and Peace, through Jesus Christ our Lord. Great and manifold were the blessings, most dread Sovereign, which Almighty God, the Father of all mercies, bestowed upon us the people of England, when first he sent Your Majesty's Royal Person to rule and reign over us. For whereas it was the expectation of many, who wished not well unto our Sion, that upon the setting of that bright *Occidental Star*, Queen *Elizabeth* of most happy memory, some thick and palpable clouds of darkness would so have overshadowed this Land, that men should have been in doubt, which we they were to walk; and that it should hardly be known, who was to direct the unsettled State. The appearance of Your Majesty, as of the *Sun* in it's strength, instantly dispelled those supposed and surmised mists, and gave unto all that were well affected exceeding cause of comfort; especially when we beheld the Government established in Your Highness, and Your hopeful Seed, by an undoubted Title, and this also accompanied with peace and tranquillity at home and abroad."

"But among all our joys, there was no one that more filled our hearts, than the blessed continuance of the preaching of God's sacred Word among us; which is that inestimable treasure, which excelleth all the riches of the earth; because the fruit thereof extendeth itself, not only to the time spent in this transitory world, but directeth and disposeth men unto that eternal happiness which is above in heaven."

"Then not to suffer this to fall to the ground, but rather to take it up, and to continue it in that state, wherein the famous Predecessor of Your Highness did leave it: nay, to go forward with the confidence and resolution of a Man in maintaining the truth of Christ, and propagating it far and near, is that which hath so bound and firmly knit the hearts of all Your Majesty's loyal and religious people unto You, that your very name is precious among them: their eye doth behold You with comfort, and they bless You in their hearts, as that sanctified Person, who, under God, is the immediate Author of their true happiness. And this their contentment doth not diminish or decay, but every day increaseth and taketh strength, when they observe, that the zeal of Your Majesty toward the house of God doth not slack or go backward, but is more and more kndled, manifesting itself abroad in the farthest parts of *Christendom*, by writing in defence of the Truth, (which hath given such a blow unto that man of sin, as will not be healed,) and every day at home, by religious and learned discourse, by frequenting the house of God, by hearing the Word preached, by cherishing the Teachers thereof, by caring for the Church, as a most tender and loving nursing Father."

"There are infinite arguments of this right Christian and religious affection in Your Majesty; but none is more forcible to declare it to others than the vehement and perpetuated desire of accomplishing and publishing of this work, which now with all humility we present unto Your Majesty. For when Your Highness has once out of deep judgment apprehended how convenient it was, that out of the Original Sacred Tongues, together with comparing of the labours, both in our own, and other foreign Languages, of many worthy men who went before us, there should be one more exact Translation of the holy Scriptures into the *English Tongue*; Your Majesty did never desist to urge and to excite those to whom it was commended, that the work might be hastened, and that the business might be expedited in so decent a manner, as a matter of such importance might justly require."

"And now at last, by the mercy of God, and the continuance of our labours, it being brought unto such a conclusion, as that we have great hopes that the Church of *England* shall reap good fruit therby; we hold it our duty to offer it to Your Majesty, not only as to our King and Soverign, but as to the principal Mover and Author of the work: humbly craving of Your most Sacred Majesty, that since things of this quality have ever been subject to the censures of illmeaning and discontented person, it may receive approbation and patronage from so learned and judicious a Prince as Your Highness is, whose allowance and acceptance of our labours shall more honour and encourage us, than all the calumniations and hard interpretations of other men shall dismay us. So that if, on the one side, we shall be traduced by Popish Persons at home or abroad, who therefore will malign us, because we are poor instruments to make God's holy Truth to be yet more and more known unto the people, whom they desire still to keep in ignorance and darkness; or if, on the other side, we shall be maligned by selfconceited Brethren, who run their own ways, and give liking unto nothing, but what is framed by themselves, and hammered on their anvil; we may rest secure, supported within by the truth and innocency of a good conscience, having walked the ways of simplicity and integrity, as before the Lord; and sustained without by the powerful protection of Your Majesty's grace and favour, which will ever give countencnace to honest and Christian endeavors against bitter censures and uncharitable imputations."

"The Lord of heaven and earth bless Your Majesty with many and happy days, that, as his heavenly hand hath enriched

Your Highness with many singular and extra- ordinary graces, happiness and true felicity, to the honour of that great GOD, and the good of his Church, through Jesus Christ our Lord and only Saviour. Amen"[2]

---

[2] *The Epistle Dedicatorie* of the King James Bible 1611.

www.ingramcontent.com/pod-product-compliance
Lightning Source LLC
Chambersburg PA
CBHW060407050426
42449CB00009B/1925